BLAST FROM THE PAST:
Idioms and Insults
(From the 1960s, 70s and Prior)

Written and Illustrated by Brigid Obrien

To my daughter, Sarah Murphy, the sunshine of my life, who I am extremely
proud of, love deeply and who also helped me make the cover of this book!

<u>Foreword</u>:

I am a baby boomer, who grew up in a bedroom community of New York City; I also lived in the State of Florida from age 11 through 15.

Depending on what part of the USA in which a person was raised, some of the phrases in this book may or may not be familiar.

My plan here is to share and document these phrases, slang, metaphors, idioms and more, for posterity. Some idioms are from my grandparents' day and older, but mostly these are from my teenage years and twenties, the 1960 and 70s.

As the years have marched on, I realized that many of these phrases are no longer used; some are, but many are not.

I hope you will enjoy my mildly humorous little book!

1. On the Lam *(Hiding from the law)*
2. He has a lame rap *(He doesn't know how to talk to a potential romantic partner.)*
3. He got a bum rap *(Unfair punishment or jail sentence)*
4. There's a rug on his head   *(He is wearing a toupee)*
5. I've been through the mill   *(I have been worked over roughly, been through a lot)*
6. Let's do it to it   *(Let's get moving on this.)*
7. Let's get it on   *(Could mean to have sex or could be applied to anything... getting ready for a project, you could say "let's get it on.")*
8. Get a move on   *(Get going on something; stop being slow or lazy about it.)*
9. Put the moves on someone   *(Flirting with intensity)*
10. Nature is calling   *(I have to go to the bathroom.)*
11. Going to see Mrs. Murphy   *(Going to the public bathroom)*
12. Sent up the river   *(Went to jail or reform school. This started in the 1890s, referring to Sing Sing prison, 30 miles north of New York City. In time, it was used to refer to any prison. In Florida, in the 1960s, teenagers would say "sent up," referring to kids who were sentenced to reform school.)*

13. I'll bet you dollars to doughnuts   *(Dollars are valuable but doughnuts are not. Short odds)*

14. Well, touch you! *(Well aren't you so special, or at least you think yo are.)*

15. Drop a dime   *(Tip off the cops. In the old days, a public telephone call cost ten cents, even when the cost went to 25 cents, the phrase didn't change.)*

16. I'll be there in two shakes of a lamb's tail   *(Sometimes said simply a "two shakes." It means very fast.)*

17. The eagle flies on Friday   *(I get paid on Friday. From the song "Stormy Monday." There is an eagle on the dollar bill and on pay day it flies into your hand.)*

18. He gave me a bum steer   *(An idiom meaning he gave me the wrong information)*

19. Gadzooks!   *(Expression of surprise or dismay)*

20. I got my wagon fixed   *(Had sexual intercourse)*

21. Got laid   *(Had sexual intercourse)*

22. I got my pipes cleaned   *(Had sexual intercourse)*

23. She frosted her hair   *(Before highlights were ever heard of, in the late 1960s we had frosting, which were chunks of blonde hair. Hair was pulled through a cap with a crochet needle and bleached.)*

24. He got frosted   *(He got drunk.)*

25. That just frosts my ass   *(Makes me mad)*

26. We got bombed   *(We got extremely drunk.)*

27. She can talk the balls off a brass monkey   *(It sounds dirty, but the brass monkey is something from an ancient ship, used to hold cannonballs. When someone talks too much, it is said they could talk those balls off the brass monkey.)*

28. He talked a blue streak!   *(He never shut up. The blue streak is referencing a lightning bolt.)*

29. He streaked around the neighborhood   *(He ran naked.)*

30. You have some brass balls   *(Slang meaning that you have excessive self assurance.)*

31. Groovy   *(From the hippie era of the 60s and 70s, but hippies I knew rarely used this term, which means that something is really cool. Hippies also did not refer to themselves as "hippies." It was a media-created term.)*

32. That is peachy keen   *(That is just great.)*

33. I will repeat it until I'm blue in the face   *(I will say this over and over until I'm low on oxygen)*

34. He is a Casper Milquetoast   *(From a comic strip in 1924 "The Timid Soul")*

35. Be there or be square   *(you want to be where the action/party/"in crowd" is)*

36. Catch you on the flip side *(Turning a vinyl record over, refers to se
    you then)*

37. Catch you on the flip flop *(Another way to say the flip side)*

38. That's boss   *(That is very cool.)*

39. Go pound sand up your ass   *(A humorous and rude way of saying g
    away)*

40. Never darken my door again   *(Do not come back)*

41. That and 50 cents will get you on the subway   *(Implies that what y
    just bragged about knowing is worthless.)*

42. What in Sam Hill? *(The initials "SH" to substitute for saying shit, a
    bad word)*

43. Frig or frigate or frig it, friggin' *(Instead of saying the F word.
    Frigate is a ship)*

44. A penny for your thoughts   *(Would love to know what you're
    thinking)*

45. Knocked up *(Pregnant)*

46. Bumped *up* *(Pregnant)*

47. Straight up *(An alcoholic drink with no ice.)*

48. Give it to me straight   *(Tell me something without the BS.)*

49. Cool out *(Relax)*

50. Chill out *(Relax)*

51. Take a chill pill *(RELAX already)*

52. Stuck your foot in your mouth *(Said something you shouldn't have)*

53. Change feet and chew vigorously *(Said something you shouldn't have said, so badly that you might as well stick the other foot in and just chew)*

54. Stepped in shit *(Got lucky or fortunate)*

55. Got lucky *(Got laid)*

56. Uptight *(Wound up, not relaxed)*

57. Your bad self *(Your authentic self, the real you)*

58. Get down *(Lose your inhibitions)*

59. Get off *(Have an orgasm; get high on a drug)*

60. Don't have a cow *(Don't get upset.)*

61. Cowabunga *(Surfer's expression of delight)*

62. Bad boy(s) *(Awesome or impressive car, boobs)*

63. Outta sight *(Really cool)*

64. Stick it in your ear *(a tricky way of not saying to stick in your REAR, a play on the words)*

65. Stick it in your left ear and blow it out your ass *(Taking "stick it in your ear" a step further)*

66. Don't have a conniption *(A conniption fit is a temper tantrum.)*

67. Make out *(In the 60s, 70s, 80s, it meant to kiss and explore maybe second base. In the 30s and 40s it meant to have sexual intercourse)*

68. The old paper bag   *(You figuratively put it on an unattractive face if you like the body)*

69. Double bagger   *(You figuratively put the bag on your face as well as the unattractive partner you chose, in case his bag falls off)*

70. Coyote ugly   *(You have sex with someone who is hard to look at, when you are presumably inebriated and the next morning you chew your arm off so you don't wake the person up.)*

71. Spacey   *(Not focused, probably in a dream world)*

72. Spaced out   *(Not focused, probably in a dream world)*

73. Space cadet   *(Not focused, probably in a dream world)*

74. Planet Clare   *(So unfocused that you are seemingly on another plane.)*

75. Space station 4   *(So unfocused that you are seemingly on your own space station)*

76. Fired up   *(Could be very angry or enthusiastic)*

77. I hear you   *(I understand what you are saying)*

78. Caught you trying to be cool   *(You think you're cool, but you're not)*

79. Calling Ralph on the porcelain telephone   *(Vomiting into the toilet)*

80. It's water under the bridge.   *(What's done is done.)*

81. Hindsight is 20-20   *(Much clearer to see what should have been done when looking back)*

82. Bah Humbug   *(Humbug goes way back over 100 years and means something fraudulent or deceitful. Ebenezer Scrooge, from the Dickens "A Christmas Carol," said Bah Humbug because he felt Christmas was a sham.)*

83. Went all the way   *(Had sexual intercourse)*

84. Rickety rickety ree, kick him in the knee! Rickety rickety rass, kick him in the other knee!   *(Preppy cheer from the 1920s)*

85. Doodly squat   *(Nothing; you've got nothing.)*

86. Diddly squat   *(Nothing; you've got nothing.)*

87. Once bitten, twice shy   *(You won't make that mistake again)*

88. If at first you don't succeed, try, try again   *(Persevere)*

89. Keep on keeping on   *(Persevere)*

90. Keep the faith   *(Persevere. Believe it will happen. Hang in there.)*

91. Rat fink   *(Tattletale)*

92. Tattletale   *(Someone who rats people out or tells on them)*

93. Rat someone out.   *(Tell on someone and get them in trouble)*

94. Nifty   *(Great, cool)*

95. Neat   *(Great, cool)*

96. Neato swifto   *(Cool x 2)*

97. Not very swift   *(Not smart)*

98. Put that in your pipe and smoke it   *(Digest what I'm saying even if you don't want to.)*

99. The elevator doesn't go to the top floor   *(Someone is missing a few thousand brain cells.)*

100. He has a screw loose   *(He is not right in the head.)*

101. The proof is in the pudding   *(You have to try something to know if it's good.)*

102. Who dresses you in the morning?   *(You seem so incompetent.)*

103. You're out to lunch or OTL   *(You are in a dream world.)*

104. I'm getting 40 winks   *(I am getting some sleep.)*

105. I didn't sleep a wink last night   *(Had a lousy night's sleep)*

106. I stuck up for you today. They said you weren't fit to eat with the pigs and I said you were.   *(Just something my grandfather used to say.)*

107. FU and the horse you rode in on   *(In case FU isn't enough, let's extend it to the horse who brought you here.)*

108. FU and the horse your grandmother rode in on   *(In case FU isn't enough, let's make it a bigger insult and direct it to you and the horse who brought granny here.)*

109. Get off your high horse   *(Stop acting like you are superior to everyone.)*

110. Your mother!   *(Teenagers would just name all the relatives, your father, your sister, your brother… no words would follow but you should understand they were insulting your mother)*

111. Your father! *(Teenagers would just name all the relatives… no words would follow but you should understand they were insulting your father)*

112. Your sister! *(Teenagers would just name all the relatives… no words would follow but you should understand they were insulting your family.)*

113. Your brother! *(Teenagers would just name all the relatives… no words would follow but you should understand they were insulting your family, going on down from mother, father, sister, brother.)*

114. Made you look *(Tricking someone to look at something that's not there. Very dumb, but kids used to say it all the time.)*

115. Go to hell in a handbasket *(Go to hell. In the days of guillotines, heads were caught in handbaskets.)*

116. Where did you get your license? Gimbel's? *(You must have bought your license because you can't drive.)*

117. You're the bee's knees *(In the 1800s, it referred to something that didn't exist. It morphed to mean something very impressive.)*

118. Leave a patch *(Screech the tires and leave a patch of rubber.)*

119. Lay a patch *(Screech the tires and leave a patch of rubber.)*

120. What's your bag? *(What are you about; what is your problem?)*

121. Dough *(Money)*

122. Bread *(Money)*

123. That's heavy   *(That's an intense bit of info)*

124. L 7   *(Put the L and 7 together and you have a square.)*

125. Square   *(Not cool, not hip)*

126. Square business   *(I am leveling with you)*

127. You are square with me   *(You have paid me back. You don't ow*
    me anything.)

128. I took a cotton to you   *(I like you.)*

129. Pull rank   *(Use your authority over someone)*

130. You look like 10 miles of bad road to a weary traveler   *(You look*
    worn out.)

131. You look like a million bucks; all green and wrinkly   *(At first this*
    sounds like a compliment and then, whoops.)

132. Who did it and ran? *(You look like you've been roughed up.)*

133. Who did it and why bother?   *(You look like you've been roughed*
    up, but why would anyone even bother doing that to the likes of you.

134. To a fare-thee-well   *(Something done to an extensive degree)*

135. Stop doing the fol-de-rol   *(Goes back possibly to Shakespeare's*
    time, but used in the early 1800s as a refrain in songs, nonsensical,
    like "lalalala." My mother used to say it when we were wasting tim

136. First day on the new feet?   *(You seem to be unfamiliar with your*
    footing, klutz.)

137. What are you looking at? Not much.   *(A rude retort for the question when someone catches you staring at them)*

138. I wouldn't F him/her with your ___ *(No way would I have sex with that person, even with YOUR private parts.)*

139. Are you writing a book? Skip that chapter.   *(You are asking too many nosey questions.)*

140. He's touched   *(He is not all there in the head.)*

141. Tough noogies   *(If you don't like it, that's too bad)*

142. I'll noogie you to death   *(I will make a fist, stick out the knuckle of the forefinger and drive it into your flesh.)*

143. If you want to dance to the music, you have to pay the piper   *(Originated with the tale, "The Pied Piper of Hamelin," who was hired to rid the town of rats. When the town didn't pay him, he lured their children away. It came to mean you have to pay the price for your behavior.)*

144. She set her cap for him   *(She targeted her desired man. When she saw him coming, she would set her cap or hat to look pretty.)*

145. Who died and made you boss?   *(Why are you bossing me around?)*

146. Okay, Big Boss Tweed   *(You're being bossy. Boss Tweed was a corrupt New York City politician in the late 1800s. He died in jail.)*

147. Do you have a match? *(Yeah! Your face to my ass)*

148. Do you have a match?   *(Not since Superman died)*

149. It's your nickel   *(In the 1950s, a making a call from a public payphone was 5 cents. If the person was wondering why you called them, they'd say "it's your nickel!" In later years when it went up to a dime and then a quarter, the saying was still "It's your nickel.")*

150. The whole kit and caboodle   *(Everything. A caboodle is a lot or collection.)*

151. She could go through the eye of a needle   *(She is too thin.)*

152. Put it where the sun don't shine   *(Put in up your arse)*

153. Have a nice trip; see you next fall   *(Just a silly thing to say when someone trips – a play on words to make it sound like vacation – and the fall season, but no – you tripped and you might fall)*

154. Go scratch   *(British origin, you say it to dismiss or refuse someone. You won't do what they've asked, so you tell them "go scratch.")*

155. You're making a mountain out of a molehill   *(You are making a big deal out of a tiny issue.)*

156. Pardon me sir, you've obviously mistaken me for someone who gives a shit.   *(I don't care about whatever you are talking about)*

157. Bite me   *(I don't like you)*

158. Eat me   *(I don't like you, vulgar)*

159. A stitch in time, saves 9   *(A quick repair now, will save more work later.)*

160. Don't count your chickens before they've hatched   *(Don't spend the money until it's in hand.)*

161. Don't beat around the bush   *(Get to the point)*

162. Make hay while the sun shines   (Get the work done)

163. FCK – the only thing missing is you   *(Cute way of being a dork asking for sex)*

164. Go fly a kite   *(Get lost)*

165. Dang! *(Attempting to avoid the religious profanity of the word "damn.")*

166. What in tarnation? *(Wondering aloud, trying not to say "damnation.")*

167. Dagnabit   *(Avoiding the religious profanity of "god damnit" and saying this in it's place)*

168. Jiminy Cricket! (This was a Disney character, but the expression is an exclamation of surprise, using the initials of "JC," which is a form of religious profanity, or avoiding exclaiming "Jesus Christ!" depending on how you look at it.

169. Jeepers Creepers   *(A minced oath, similar to Jiminy Cricket. Avoiding religious profanity of exclaiming "Jesus Christ.")*

170. An apple a day keeps the doctor away. *(Prevent disease by healthy eating)*

171. An ounce of prevention is worth a pound of cure *(Easier to prevent something than try to fix it)*

172. No point closing the barn door after the horse has gotten out *(the damage is done; you can't go backwards in time to prevent it)*

173. He has egg on his face *(appearing ridiculous because of foolish actions)*

174. Sleazeball *(A sleazy person)*

175. Sleazebag *(A sleazy person)*

176. Scumbag   *(A used condom; that is how low you think of the person you call this name.)*

177. Scum bucket   *(Same as scumbag, only overflowing with scum)*

178. You're preaching to the choir *(I'm already on your side so stop trying to pitch to me)*

179. Pissing against the tide   *(up against monumental obstacles)*

180. Don't cry wolf *(from the fairy tale – you cry for help for phony reasons and when you really are in need, everyone thinks you're a faker)*

181. It's colder than a witch's teat   *(It is very cold)*

182. It's colder than a landlord's heart   *(It is very cold)*

183. Dead as a doornail   *(No life in a doornail)*

184. Dead ringer *(Means you look exactly like someone. The term "ringer" comes from "ring," which was an old-fashioned term for switching something identical in order to deceive.)*

185. Ringer *(An imposter)*

186. Greek to me *(Might as well be in a foreign language because I don't understand it)*

187. He is as Irish as Paddy's pig *(Someone looks very Irish)*

188. He has the map of Ireland on his face   *(Someone looks very Irish)*

189. He's a putz   *(A useless person)*

190. Putzing around   *(Wasting time on unproductive activities)*

191. He's a real schmuck *(A jerk)*

192. Putana *(Whore)*

193. Son of a seacook   *(Avoiding the profanity of "son of a bitch")*

194. Son of a bitch   *(An exclamation of surprise good or bad; a vulgar term for a person you are angry with)*

195. I'm gonna smack you upside your head   *(Just what it sounds like)*

196. Did someone step on a duck?   *(Did someone pass gas?)*

197. Who cut the cheese?   *(Who farted?)*

198. Who cut the limburger?   *(Who passed the extremely smelly gas; limburger is a cheese with a most foul odor.)*

199. Doofy   *(Not very smart, but nerdy)*

200. Porking   *(A vulgar expression for having sexual intercourse)*

201. Dufus/Doofus   *(A person who appears to be not very smart)*

202. Dork   *(Goofy person)*

203. Take a hike   *(Go away for a long walk)*

204. Take a long walk off a short pier   *(Take a long walk and get away from me, but make it take longer by jumping into some water.)*

205. Go jump in the lake   *(Go away. This isn't a fun swimming expression. This is like "jump in with your clothes on and don't bother me for a long time.")*

206. It doesn't amount to a hill of beans   *(Beans being so cheap that even a pile of them is worth nothing.)*

207. What does that have to do with the price of rice in China?   *(What you are saying has no relevance to anything in this conversation.)*

208. Greaser   *(A man who slicks his hair back with grease, a la Elvis)*

209. Grease monkey   *(Someone who works on cars a lot)*

210. I gave him the *raspberry*   *(That is when you stick your tongue out little and blow, to make a silly sound and show displeasure)*

211. I gave him the Bronx Cheer   *(Same as the raspberry. That is when you stick your tongue out a little and blow, to make a silly noise and show displeasure.)*

212. He popped my cherry   *(He took my virginity.)*

213. Not my cup of tea   *(That doesn't suit me)*

214. Make a mess   *(In the south, this is a big salad of greens. My friend's mother, who was from Texas, used to make a mess for us.)*

215. Tickle your fancy   *(It means you like something)*

216. Tickle your innards   *(Make you laugh deeply)*

217. I'm hip to it   *(I know what is happening. I'm in on it.)*

218. That's just ducky *(That is a term of admiration that goes back to the early 1800s)*

219. Shit on a shingle   *(Creamed chipped beef on toast)*

220. Jack and Jill on a raft   *(Poached eggs on toast)*

221. Well shiver me timbers!   *(Timbers is a slang term for legs, so this means your legs are trembling)*

222. You're a dipshit   *(You are just a fool)*

223. As an idiot he's flawless   *(He's an absolutely perfect idiot.)*

224. Well I'll be dipped in shit!   *(I am truly amazed at something.)*

225. I'll be doggone *(Avoiding the religious profanity of "I'll be God damned.")*

226. Doggone it!   *(Avoiding the religious profanity of "God damnit.")*

227. Fixed you up!   *(Set you up on a blind date)*

228. Cheese it! The cops!   *(Let's get out of here; cops are coming!)*

229. The life of Reilly   *(The easy life)*

230. Do me a solid   *(Do me a favor)*

231. Yellow bellied   *(Coward)*

232. Chicken   *(Scared)*

233. Chicken shit   *(You're a coward and scared)*

234. Chicken out   *(Lose your nerve)*

235. Turd burglar   *(Someone who engages in anal sex)*

236. Spiffy   *(Dressed up)*

237. Spiffed up   *(Dressed up)*

238. Gussied up   *(Dressed up)*

239. Built like a brick shithouse   *(Has a good physique)*

240. She is stacked   *(She has very big breasts.)*

241. She is busty   *(She has very big breasts.)*

242. Got your pipes cleaned   *(Engaged in sexual intercourse)*

243. It's not the size of the sea; it's the motion of the ocean *(It doesn't matter how large a man's penis is if he has a technique to please a woman.)*

244. You wouldn't buy a pig in a poke, would you?   *(You should inspect something thoroughly before making a purchase.)*

245. Hang loose, Mother Goose   *(Relax, but saying it in a fun way that rhymes)*

246. Walk much?   *(This is what you say if you want to be rude when someone trips)*

247. Talk much?   *(This is a rude thing to say when someone gets tongue tied)*

248. Tongue tied   *(Stumbles over words, can't find the right words)*

249. First day on the new feet? *(This is a rude or possibly humorous thing to say when someone trips.)*

250. Get on the quick foot   *(Get going and give yourself an edge by using the "quick foot.")*

251. Get on the good foot   *(Get going and give yourself an edge by using the "good foot.")*

252. From jump street   *(From the very beginning)*

253. From the giddy up   *(From the very beginning)*

254. From the get go   *(From the very beginning)*

255. Johnson Bar   *(Slang for a man's penis; it is a long control lever on a locomotive.)*

256. Prick   *(Slang for a man's penis. Someone who is being very mean is a prick or a dick.)*

257. Shove it   *(Put it up your anus. In other words – someone very much dislikes what you are saying or doing.)*

258. Shove it sideways   *(Put it up your anus, but this time do it sideways so it's uncomfortable. In other words – someone very much dislikes what you are saying or doing.)*

259. Stuff it   *(Put it up your anus. In other words – someone very much dislikes what you are saying or doing.)*

260. Cram it   *(Same as "stuff it," but with more oomph)*

261. Get stuffed   *(Similar to "shove it" or "stuff it")*

262. Get bent   *(Slang from the 1960s, could mean for a man to bend his penis; it's a rude dismissive statement.)*

263. Don't get bent out of shape   *(Don't get overly mad or upset over things.)*

264. Up yours   *(Put it up your anus. In other words – someone very much dislikes what you are saying or doing.)*

265. Put it where the sun don't shine   *(Put it up your anus. In other words – someone very much dislikes what you are saying or doing.)*

266. She's got freckles on her BUT… she's nice   *(Just a silly thing my dad used to say)*

267. Peanut sat on the railroad track, his heart was all aflutter. Along came a choo-choo train. Toot toot! Peanut butter.   *(Another silly thing that my dad used to say)*

268. If you can't take the heat, get out of the kitchen   *(Toughen up or get out.)*

269. You're too big for your britches   *(You are very impressed with yourself, and it's blown out of proportion.)*

270. Gee whiz   *(An exclamation of surprise or disbelief. Also thought to be a euphemistic alteration of the word "Jesus." The nuns who taught me would not allow us to say "gee" for this reason.)*

271. Gee willikers   *(An exclamation of surprise or disbelief, like saying "gosh." Also thought to be a euphemistic alteration of the word "Jesus." The nuns who taught me would not allow us to say "gee" for this reason.)*

272. Get a grip   *(Control yourself)*

273. That's the name of that tune   *(That's the way it is.)*

274. Put your thinking cap on   *(Figure it out)*

275. Why buy the cow when you can get the milk for free? *(In the olden days, they thought a woman should hold back sex until marriage. If you gave up your virginity, why would someone have to marry you. Women should hold back sex, but not men. Popular saying before the days of birth control pills, which became available around 1969.)*

276. Get off the table Mabel; the dollar is for the beer   *(A silly phrase my friend's dad learned in the Navy in WWII)*

277. Ask me   *(Ask me if I care, because I don't.)*

278. Ask me if I care   *(I do not care.)*

279. Tell me about it   *(I completely agree and/or already know what you're talking about.)*

280. Tell me something I don't know   *(You are telling me very old news)*

281. Go tell someone who gives a shit   *(I don't care what you have to say.)*

282. I don't give a rat's ass   *(I don't care what you have to say.)*

283. I don't give a tinker's dam   *(People think it's "I don't give a*

damn," but the real saying is that you don't give a dam – not damn.

tinker's dam is a tiny thing, like the dam a dentist puts in your mou

It makes sense that if you don't give a dam, you care very little.)

284. 50,000 Frenchmen can't be wrong   *(This is from a 1929 Broadw*

show of the same name. It meant "don't condemn me for my

lifestyle," but later became a blanket statement for anything where

large group had a belief to back you up.)

285. He got his ears lowered   *(He got a haircut.)*

286. You can't polish a turd   *(You can try to make something more*

appealing or get plastic surgery or fudge numbers, but some things

are too bad to fix.)

287. Good morning glory, how dee dew drop?   *(Something my*

grandfather said to me every morning)

288. Shot at and missed, shit on and hit   *(You say this after an*

exhausting day)

289. Tighter than a crab's ass   *(A cheapskate)*

290. No dice   *(We don't have a deal.)*

291. Don't change horses in the middle of the stream   *(don't alter your*

course of action or your leader in the middle of a project, don't

change your mind at an inopportune moment.)

292. Are you going to the movies? I thought I saw you picking your seat. *(This is a funny/rude comment to say when you see someone pulling at the back of their pants.)*

293. You can't have your cake and eat it too *(You can't have it both ways.)*

294. Don't cry over spilt milk *(What's done is done)*

295. If the shoe fits, wear it *(Perhaps what you are saying about someone else, really applies to yourself.)*

296. One bad apple can spoil the whole barrel. *(One person can be a bad influence on the group. The Jackson Five song said the opposite.)*

297. Bad apple *(Someone in a group who makes problems)*

298. Don't stir the pot. *(Don't make things worse)*

299. Is that a "needy bump"? *(A pimple on your face, supposedly from lack of sex)*

300. Goody Two Shoes *(always follows rules, little miss perfect)*

301. She's a real Pollyanna *(Over-the-top optimism, always sees the good in people to an annoying degree)*

302. Run like the dickens *(The word "dickens" was used in olden days in place of the word "devil.")*

303. You dirty stay out *(Someone who goes to a bar or party and doesn't come home until the next morning.*

304. Via air mail   *(From 1918 to 1975 air mail was sold as a separate service through the US Post Office. There were envelopes you could buy that said "par avion" or "via air mail." There were also stamps for air mail that cost more than "surface mail.")*

305. He has a bug up his ass   *(Something is bothering him)*

306. He is bugging out   *(He is going crazy)*

307. That was wicked!   *(Although "wicked" means evil, literally, this is also a colloquialism meaning something was really great.)*

308. Bug off   *(Leave me alone.)*

309. Bugger off   *(British version of "leave me alone")*

310. MYOB   *(Mind Your Own Business. This was a favorite of my sixth grade teacher, a nun named Sister Mary Dionysia.)*

311. Busted   *(You got caught.)*

312. She's got the goods on them   *(Evidence that they did something wrong)*

313. You're a dickfour. What's a dickfour?   *(Self explanatory)*

314. Buzz off   *(Get out of here.)*

315. I got buzzed   *(I got drunk/stoned.)*

316. He is AC/DC   *(In electricity, it's alternating current, direct current. In slang, it means you go both ways, bisexual.)*

317. You better haul ass!   *(Hurry up!)*

318. Long in the tooth   *(Old)*

319. Don't stand on ceremony   *(Don't insist on following formalities.)*

320. Get down   *(Lose your inhibitions and enjoy yourself.)*

321. Meat market   *(A bar where people go to get picked up or meet the opposite sex)*

322. I want to get next to you   *(I want to be intimate.)*

323. Don't let her get next to you   *(Don't let her bother you or get under your skin)*

324. Let her stew in her juices   *(Let her marinate in her own anger.)*

325. The lights are on, but nobody's home   *(Not much going on in that brain.)*

326. I looked in the want ads   *(In the old days, the "want ads" was a section in classified where you could find jobs under "help wanted.")*

327. Let it all hang out   *(Relax, be yourself without caring what others think.)*

328. Onion skin   *(Very thin paper that was commonly used on a typewriter. It is still available for different purposes, such as origami and crafts.)*

329. Flower power   *(Hippies or flower children, promotion of peace and love)*

330. Flower children   *(Hippies)*

331. I am a human being; please do not fold, spindle or mutilate
(A popular slogan back in the 60s, printed on a campaign style
pin/button)

332. Carbon paper *(Before copy machines, you would put carbon paper*
in between sheets of plain paper so that when you typed, you had
duplicates or triplicates.)

333. Correctype *(Little strips of white substance that you would put on*
your error in the typewriter. Strike the error again and the white on
the paper would remove the typo. This was before "White Out" was
invented.)

334. Dressed to the nines *(In the middle ages, there were 9 "worthies,*
examples of well-dressed men. It means to be dressed extravagantly)

335. Face the music *(Thought to have originated in the mid-nineteenth*
century when speaking of stage fright, it means to face the
consequences and accept responsibility.)

336. Kick the bucket *(To die. Originated when people sadly committed*
suicide by making a noose and then standing on the bucket.)

337. His nose was out of joint *(Reacted with hurt feelings)*

338. Beat the daylights out of you *(In the old days, they would "beat the*
daylight into you" by injuring you so much that the light would shine
through you. Somehow it morphed into beating the daylights out of
you.)

339. Things are going to the dogs   *(Worsening)*

340. Don't that jar your preserves?!   *(An exclamation, upon seeing something remarkable)*

341. I know how to get his goat   *(I know how to make him angry.)*

342. He rubbed me the wrong way   *(He irked, irritated or vexed me.)*

343. No shit, Sherlock!   *(It's obvious – sarcastically saying "you're a great detective.")*

344. Put on your rubbers   *(Rubber shoe coverings that people commonly wore in the rain. Lost popularity in the late 1960s, but still available today.)*

345. Use a rubber   *(A rubber is a condom.)*

346. A motley crew   *(A group of mismatched people. Origins from a few centuries ago when motley was a cloth of more than one color.)*

347. When pigs fly   *(It's never going to happen.)*

348. Flim flam   *(A con game. "Don't flim flam me.")*

349. Come to my crib   *(My house or apartment)*

350. Come to my pad   *(My house or apartment)*

351. Sexpot   *(A sexy person, but usually a glamorous celebrity with enormous sex appeal)*

352. Duck's Ass or DA   *(A duck's ass was a popular man's hairstyle*
the 50s. Think of the Fonz. The hair was long and slicked back wit
some greasy pomade. In the back it came together from both sides,
resembling a duck's rear end.)

353. Deep 6 it.   *(End it, get rid of it. Origins seem to be from the Nav*
in WWI. It was meant to throw it overboard at about 6 fathoms.)

354. Eight-six it.   *(Similar to "deep 6 it.") It means to end or*
permanently get rid of something. There are so many theories on h
this saying started, from the 86ᵗʰ precinct in NYC to the filter on col
film, that I don't think we can pin it down. It is used in restaurants
lot. Instead of saying "we are out of chicken salad, you would say
the chicken salad.'")

355. Hot diggity or hot diggity dog *(Expression of excitement or deligh*

356. By and by *(Eventually, an unspecified time. We will go on vacati*
by-and-by.)

357. Leaf through the pages *(Flip through without really focusing on t*
content. The word "page" comes from the Latin word "pagina,"
which means a written page, leaf, sheet.)

358. Bit the dust *(Passed away)*

359. Kicked the bucket *(Passed away)*

360. Newfangled *(Recently made, but not always an improvement)*

361. Frills and fallalery (*Flashy or cheap trimmings. I've no time for your frills and fallalery.*)

362. Derring-do (*Being bold in a foolish way*)

363. Toute suite (*French phrase for "in a hurry." You better get that done toute suite!*)

364. Outta sight (*Really cool*)

365. Uptight (*Wound up, not relaxed.*)

366. Sing for your supper (*Roots of this phrase come from the wandering minstrels who would sing in exchange for a meal. Nowadays it means work for your pay.*)

367. Nerts to you! (*Annoyance, exasperation or disgust*)

368. Various and sundry (*Miscellaneous. The term "sundry" means variety. There used to be "sundry shops" where you would buy small incidental things.*)

369. Put a load in your cigarette (*We used to have small things, called "loads," that we would insert into the tobacco at the end of a friend's cigarette. When they lit the cigarette, there would be a small explosion, which was lots of fun back then.*)

370. Cut the mustard (*To succeed or come up to expectations.*)

371. Shake your money maker (*To use your sexual assets to get what you want*)

372. Tempest in a teapot. *(A small event that has been blown out of proportion)*

373. Can you dig it? *(Do you understand? Are you cool with that?)*

374. Mollycoddle *(To baby, pamper, indulge someone)*

375. Almost doesn't count; only in horseshoes and hand grenades.

376. All over me like a cheap suit (or a new suite)   *(overly attracted to a thing or person. Too close.)*

377. All over me like glue on a shoe   *(overly attracted to a thing or person. Too close.)*

378. All over me like white on rice   ) *(overly attracted to a thing or person. Too close.)*

379. All over it like flies on sh--   ) *(overly attracted to a thing or person. Too close.)*

380. Cramp my style. *(Restricts my actions and freedom)*

381. Jones-ing. *(To have a hankering for something or an addiction.)* Legend has it that Jones Alley in Manhattan was a haven for drug addicts many years ago and hence the term, Jonesing.

382. Flip your lid. *(Lose your mind.)* *"Lid" is also a slang word for a* hat.

383. Nincompoop. *(An idiot)* This word goes back to the 1600s in the English language. It is thought to be derived from "non compos mentis" which means not of sound mind.

384. Grease you up. *(To flatter in a manipulative way.)*

385. Grease your palm. *(Make a bribe.)*

386. The rabbit died. *(You're pregnant.)* From the 1930s until the 1960s, rabbits were injected with women's urine. The misconception was that the rabbit died if you were pregnant, but in reality, they had to kill the rabbit to examine the ovaries of it for changes.

387. Keep your nose to the grindstone. *(To work hard).* This expression goes back to the 1500s, alluding to a tool that must be sharpened by holding it to a grindstone.

388. The squeaky wheel gets the grease. *(If you speak up you are more likely to get help.)*

389. Clodhoppers. *(Big clunky shoes)*

390. Copping nookie. *(Having sex)*

Photo of the author at age 3

The author at age 19, chowing down on a hamburger

Brigid Obrien is now an old bag, living in upstate New York.
Pictured here at age 60, she thought she could be
a standup comedian but failed.

The author at her 8th grade graduation with her parents, at St. Joan of Arc in Boca Raton, Florida.

The author on her wedding day, at age 20.

The marriage did not work out, but that is okay. Life is good.

www.ingramcontent.com/pod-product-compliance
Lightning Source LLC
Chambersburg PA
CBHW061741250726
48657CB00002B/1031